CW00422437

ACAB

ACAB

ACAB STRIKE! Magazine

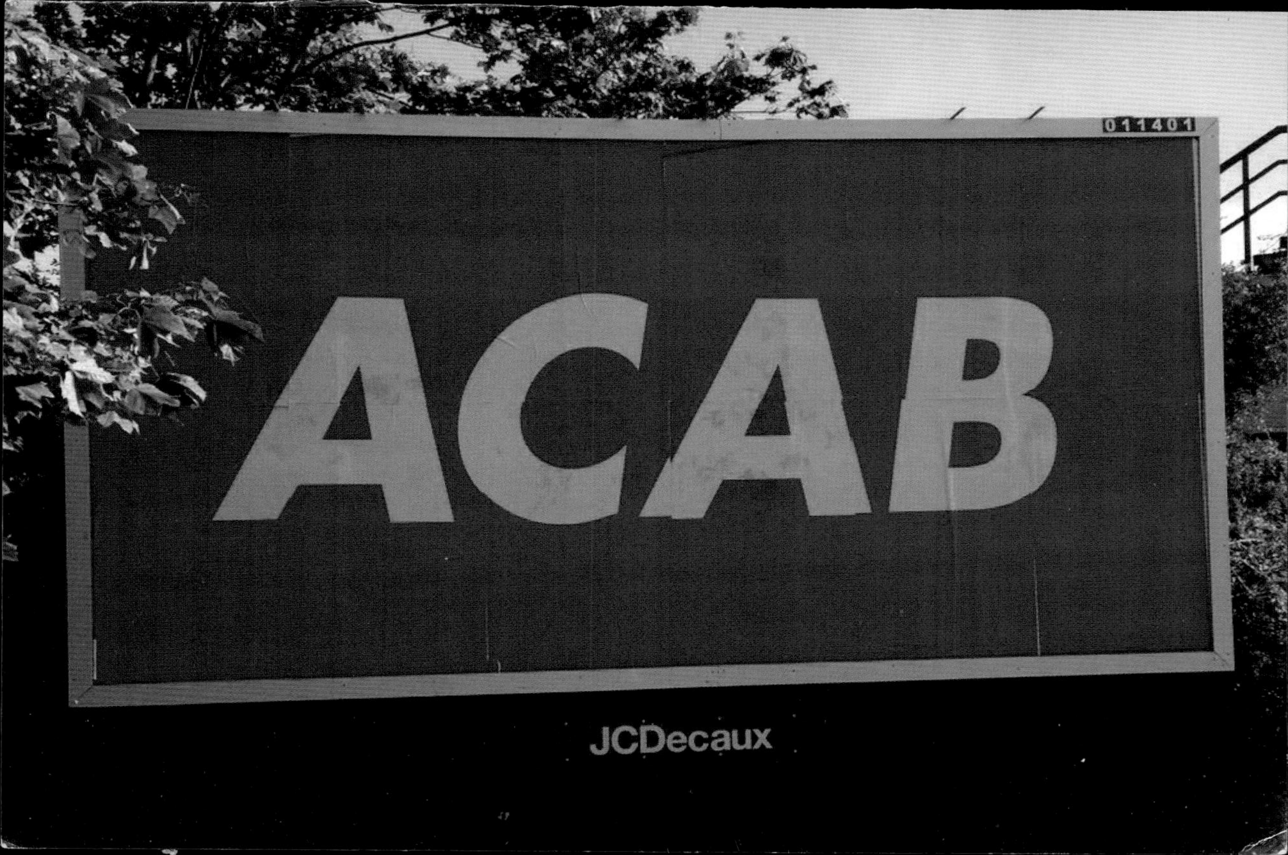
011401
ACAB
JCDecaux

GREATEST *Hits*

ACAT

Cops — Targets

All — Are

THE **POLICE**

PARENTAL ADVISORY
EXPLICIT CONTENT

Fuck The Police Hogre

GREATEST *Hits*

ACAT · Cops · Targets · All · A-B

THE ~~POLICE~~

PARENTAL ADVISORY
EXPLICIT CONTENT

No-one is Illegal Illustre Feccia

NO ONE IS ILLEGAL

EARN 25k AS A P.C.S.O

YOU'RE JUST A GRASS WITH A BADGE

METROPOLITAN POLICE

Because you just can't be trusted

Grass With A Badge Dr D

"I have no particular love for the idealised 'worker' as he appears in the bourgeois Communist's mind, but when I see an actual flesh-and-blood worker in conflict with his natural enemy, the policeman, I do not have to ask myself which side I am on."

George Orwell

Natural Enemies Hannah Meese

ACAB

"I have no particular love for the idealised 'worker' as he appears in the bourgeois Communist's mind, but when I see an actual flesh-and-blood worker in conflict with his natural enemy, the policeman, I do not have to ask myself which side I am on."

George Orwell

Bobbies on the Beatings Marco Bevilacqua

NO PEACE

NO JUSTICE

A.C.A.B.

No Justice No Peace Goldpeg

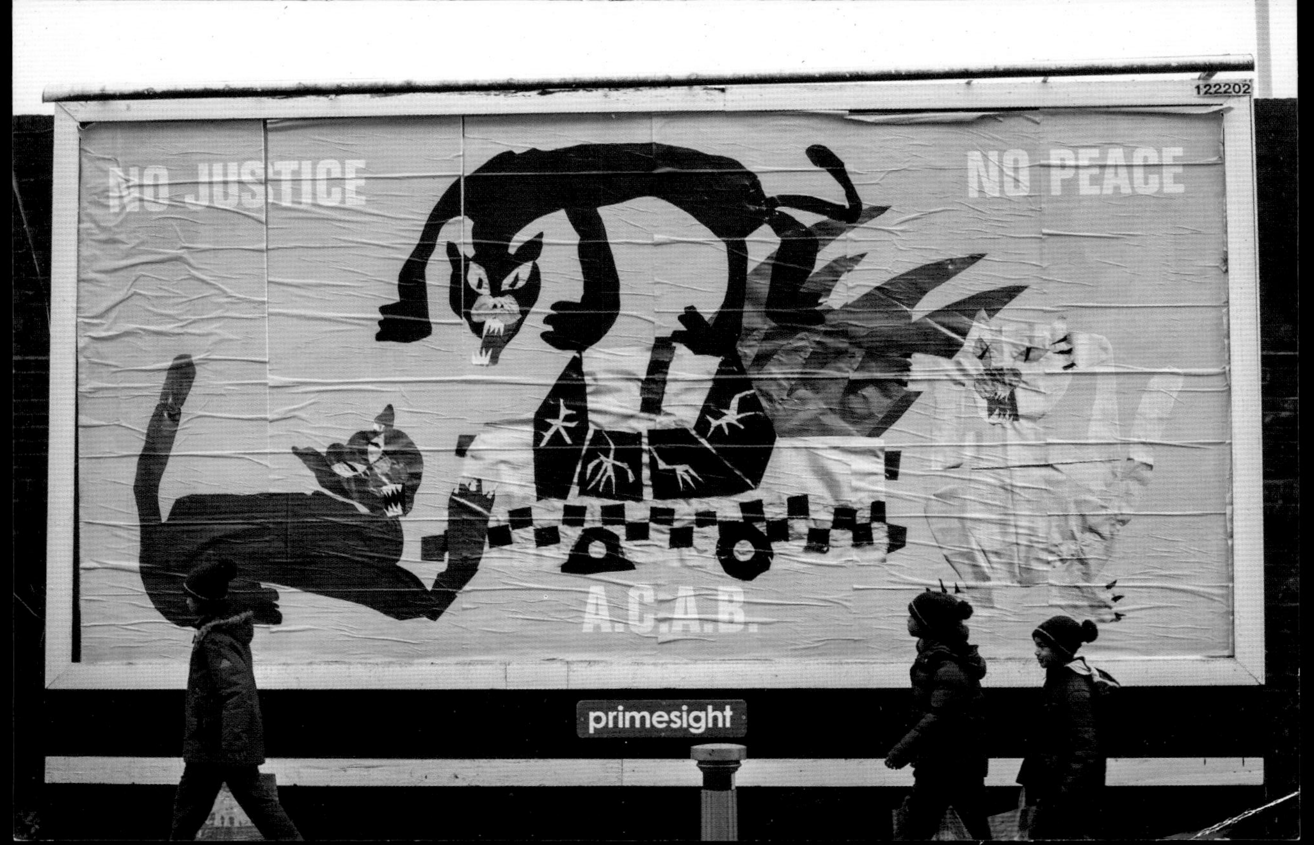
122202
NO JUSTICE
NO PEACE
A.C.A.B.
primesight

a.e.a.b.

Since 1990, 1513 people have died in police custody or following police contact.
Not a single officer has been convicted for any of their deaths.

Getting away with it since 1829
#ACAB

 METROPOLITAN POLICE **TOTAL PROPAGANDA**

Total Propaganda STRIKE! Magazine

Riot City Bill Posters/Brandalism

Just call...

WE'RE HERE
TO HELP

POLICE

ACAB: A Nursery Rhyme

Sean Bonney

 for "I love you" say fuck the police / for
"the fires of heaven" say fuck the police, don't say
"recruitment" don't say "trotsky" say fuck the police
for "alarm clock" say fuck the police
            for "my morning commute" for
"electoral system" for "endless solar wind" say fuck the police
don't say "I have lost understanding of my visions" don't say
"that much maligned human faculty" don't say
"suicided by society" say fuck the police / for "the movement
of the heavenly spheres" say fuck the police / for
"the moon's bright globe" for "the fairy mab" say
fuck the police / don't say "direct debit" don't say "join the party"
say "you are sleeping for the boss" and then say fuck the police
don't say "evening rush-hour" say fuck the police / don't say
"here are the steps I've taken to find work" say fuck the police
don't say "tall skinny latté" say fuck the police / for
"the earth's gravitational pull" say fuck the police / for
"make it new" say fuck the police
            all other words are buried there
all other words are spoken there / don't say "spare change"
say fuck the police / don't say "happy new year" say fuck the police
perhaps say "rewrite the calendar" but after that, immediately
after that say fuck the police / for "philosopher's stone" for
"royal wedding" for "the work of transmutation" for "love
of beauty" say fuck the police / don't say "here is my new poem"
say fuck the police
            say no justice no peace and then say fuck the police

#ADHACKMANIFESTO

1. ADVERTISING SHITS IN YOUR HEAD
IT IS A FORM OF VISUAL AND PSYCHOLOGICAL POLLUTION.

2. REMOVING/REPLACING/DEFACING ADVERTISING IS NOT VANDALISM
IT IS AN ACT OF TIDYING UP THAT IS BOTH LEGALLY & MORALLY DEFENSIBLE.

3. THE VISUAL REALM IS A PUBLIC REALM
IT IS PART OF THE COMMONS
IT BELONGS TO EVERYONE, SO NO-ONE SHOULD BE ABLE TO OWN IT.

4. OUTDOOR ADVERTISING CAN AND SHOULD BE BANNED
SAO PAULO DID IT IN 2007, & GRENOBLE FOLLOWED SUIT IN 2015.

Subvertising

Hogre

The constant imposition of advertising in front of our eyes is an oppressive, dictatorial and violent act.

Subvertising reacts to this visual pollution with an equally violent and direct aesthetic, without asking for permission or waiting for consensus. Removing, replacing and defacing advertising is an act of civil disobedience that is both legally and morally defensible.

First published in London, 2018 by Dog Section Press
Printed by Calverts Ltd, a workers' cooperative

ISBN 9780993543548

Layout by Matt Bonner revoltdesign.org
Dog Section Press logo by Marco Bevilacqua